1

Pa [illegible] Hood &
Jack and the Beanstalk

By Varg Vikernes & Marie Cachet

Initial Notes

This is part II in our Paganism Explained series. See Part I for an introduction to this series. This time we take a look at a few of our European Fairy Tales. Yes, these are but a few examples: There will be more of them, as well as more myths, explained in future parts of our Paganism Explained series.

Varg Vikernes
December 2017

Little Red Riding Hood

Version collected in Touraine in France by M. Légot (*Revue de l'Avranchin*, 1885):

Once there was a young girl in the countryside who heard that her grandmother was sick; she set out the next day to visit her; but when she was far away, at a crossroads, she did not know which way to take.

There she met a very ugly man, leading a sow, and to whom she asked her way, telling her that she was going to see visit her sick grandmother.

You have to go to the left, he says, it's the best and the shortest way, and you'll soon arrive. The girl went there; but the road was the longest and the worst; she took a long time to reach her grandmother's house, and it was with great difficulty that she arrived there very late.

While the little Jeannette was engaged in the chaos of the wrong road, the ugly man, who

had just informed her badly, went to the right by the right and short way, then he arrived at the grandmother's house long before her.
He killed the poor woman and put her blood in a bottle ("huche" in french) and went to bed.

When the little girl arrived at her grandmother's house, she knocked at the door, opened it, entered, and said: "How are you doing, grandma?"

"Not well, my daughter," responded the good-for-nothing who gave the impression that he was suffering and disguised his voice. "Are you hungry?"

"Yes, grandma. What's there to eat?"

"There's some blood in the cupboard. Take the pan and fry it. Then eat it up."

The little girl obeyed.

While she was frying the blood, she heard some voices that sounded like those of angels from the top of the chimney, and they said: "Ah! Cursed be the little girl who's frying the blood of her grandmother!"

"What are those voices saying, grandmother, those voices that are singing from the chimney?"
"Don't listen to them, my daughter, those are just little birds singing in their own language."

And the little girl continued to fry the blood of her grandmother, But the voices began again to sing: "Ah! the naughty little naughty who fries the blood of her grandmother!" Jeannette said then: "I'm not hungry, my grandmother, I do not want to eat that blood." "Well! Come to bed, my daughter, come to bed." Jeannette went to bed next to him.

When she was there, she exclaimed:

"Ah! my grandmother, why have you so big arms?"
- "It's better embrace you, my daughter, it's better to embrace you."
- "Ah! my grandmother, why have you so big legs?"
- "It is to walk better, my daughter, it is to walk better."
- "Ah! my grandmother, why have you so big eyes?"

- "It is to better see you, my daughter, it is to better see you."
- "Ah! my grandmother, why do you have such big teeth?"

- "It's better for eating my daughter, it's better for eating."

Jeannette became scared and said: "Ah! Grandmother, I've got the urge to go (i. e. "take a leak").

"Do it in bed, my daughter. Do it in bed."

"It would be too dirty, grandma! If you're afraid that I might run off, tie a rope around my leg. If you're bothered that I'm outside too long, just pull on the rope, and you can assure yourself that I'm still here."

"You're right my daughter. You're right."

- And the monster attaches a rope of wool to Jeannette's leg, then he kept the end in his hand. When the girl was outside, she cut the rope of wool and went away. A moment after the fake grandmother said: "Did you pee,

Jeannette, did you pee?" And the same voices of the little angels answered again from the top of the chimney: "Not yet, my grandmother, not yet!" But when she had been there for a long time they said: "it's over".

The monster pulled the rope, but there was no one at the other end.

This evil man got up angrily and went up on his big sow he had put on the roof and ran after the girl to catch her; he arrived at a river where washers were washing. He tells them:
"Have you seen that Tomboy girl/that boy-girl with a dog wagging its tail tagging along on this trail?"

in French:
Avez-vous vu passer fillon fillette,
Avec un chien barbette (barbet)
Qui la suivette (suivait)

The Girl and the Wolf (1874)

A Variant of the tale of the Little Red Riding Hood, told in July 1874 by Nanette Lévesque.

A little girl was at work in a house to keep two cows. When she had finished her job, she went away. Her master gave her a little cheese and a small loaf of bread.

“Here, my dear, bring it to your mother. This cheese and that loaf will be for your supper when you arrive at home.”

The girl takes the cheese and the loaf. She went into the woods and met the wolf, who said to her, "Where are you going, my dear?
- “I'm going to my mother. I finished my job.”
- “Did they pay you?”
- “Yes, they paid me, gave me a little loaf, gave me a cheese.”
- “Which side do you go to?”
- “I pass the side of the pins, and you, which side do you go?”
- “I pass on the side of the needles.”

The wolf started to run, and went to kill the mother and ate her, he ate half, he set the fire on, cooked the other half and closed the door. He went to sleep in the mother's bed.

The girl arrived. She knocked on the door: "Ah! my mother, open to me."

- "I'm sick my little one. I went to bed. I can not get up and open. Turn the handle." When the little girl turned the handle, opened the door entered the house, the wolf was in his mother's bed.

- "Are you sick, mother?"

- "Yes, I am very sick. And you came from Nostera."

- "Yes, I came. They gave me a loaf and a piece of cheese."

- "It's fine my little, give me a little piece." The wolf took the piece and ate it, and said to the girl, "there is meat on the fire and wine on the table, when you have eaten and had a drink, you will come to bed."

The wolf had put the blood of her mother in a bottle, and he had put a glass next to it, half full of blood. He said to her: "Eat meat, there is some in the pot; there is wine on the table, you will drink it."

There was a little bird on the window when the little girl ate her mother who said:

- "R tin tin tin tin. You eat your mother's meat and you drink her blood." And the little girl says:
- "What does he say mum, this bird?"

- "He says nothing, keeps eating, he has plenty of time to sing."

And when she had eaten and drunk the wolf said to the little girl: "Come to bed, little one. Come to bed. You have eaten enough my baby, now and come and lie down with me. I have cold feet you'll warm me."

- "I'm going to bed mom."
She undresses and goes to bed with her mother, saying:

- “Ah! Mom, you're gruff!”
"It's old age, my child, it's old age.”
The little girl touches her legs: “Ah! Mom your nails have become long!”
“It's old age, it's old age.”
- “Ah! Mom, your teeth have become long too!”
“It's old age, it's old age. My teeth are to eat you, and he ate her.”

Charles Perrault, "Little Red Riding Hood" (1697) Translation by Andrew Lang (1889)

Once upon a time there lived in a certain village a little country girl, the prettiest creature who was ever seen. Her mother was excessively fond of her; and her grandmother doted on her still more. This good woman had a little red riding hood made for her. It suited the girl so extremely well that everybody called her Little Red Riding Hood. One day her mother, having made some cakes, said to her, "Go, my dear, and see how your grandmother is doing, for I hear she has been very ill. Take her a cake, and this little pot of butter."

Little Red Riding Hood set out immediately to go to her grandmother, who lived in another village. As she was going through the wood, she met with a wolf, who had a very great mind to eat her up, but he dared not, because of some woodcutters working nearby in the forest. He asked her where she was going.

The poor child, who did not know that it was dangerous to stay and talk to a wolf, said to him, "I am going to see my grandmother and bring her a cake and a little pot of butter from my mother." "Does she live far off?" said the wolf "Oh I say," answered Little Red Riding Hood; "it is beyond that mill you see there, at the first house in the village." "Well," said the wolf, "and I'll go and see her too. I'll go this way and go you that, and we shall see who will be there first."

The wolf ran as fast as he could, taking the shortest path, and the little girl took a roundabout way, entertaining herself by gathering nuts, running after butterflies, and gathering bouquets of little flowers.

It was not long before the wolf arrived at the old woman's house. He knocked at the door: tap, tap. "Who's there?" "Your grandchild, Little Red Riding Hood," replied the wolf, counterfeiting her voice; "who has brought you a cake and a little pot of butter sent you by mother." The good grandmother, who was in bed, because she was somewhat ill, cried out, "Pull the bobbin, and the latch will go up." The wolf pulled the bobbin, and the door opened, and then he immediately fell upon the good woman and ate her up in a moment, for it been more than three days since he had eaten.

He then shut the door and got into the grandmother's bed, expecting Little Red Riding Hood, who came some time afterwards and knocked at the door: tap, tap. "Who's there?" Little Red Riding Hood, hearing the big voice of the wolf, was at first afraid; but believing her grandmother had a cold and was hoarse, answered, "It is your grandchild Little Red Riding Hood, who has brought you a cake and a little pot of butter mother sends you." The wolf cried out to her, softening his voice as much as he could, "Pull the bobbin, and the latch will go up." Little Red Riding Hood pulled the bobbin, and the door opened.

The wolf, seeing her come in, said to her, hiding himself under the bedclothes, "Put the cake and the little pot of butter upon the stool, and come get into bed with me." Little Red Riding Hood took off her clothes and got into bed.

She was greatly amazed to see how her grandmother looked in her nightclothes, and said to her, "Grandmother, what big arms you have!" "All the better to hug you with, my dear." "Grandmother, what big legs you have!"

"All the better to run with, my child." Grandmother, what big ears you have!" "All the better to hear with, my child." "Grandmother, what big eyes you have!" "All the better to see with, my child." "Grandmother, what big teeth you have got!" "All the better to eat you up with."

And, saying these words, this wicked wolf fell upon Little Red Riding Hood, and ate her all up.

Moral: Children, especially attractive, well bred young ladies, should never talk to strangers, for if they should do so, they may well provide dinner for a wolf. I say "wolf," but there are various kinds of wolves. There are also those who are charming, quiet, polite, unassuming, complacent, and sweet, who pursue young women at home and in the streets. And unfortunately, it is these gentle wolves who are the most dangerous ones of all.

Grimm Brothers, "Little Red Cap" from *Children's and Household Tales* (1812 - 1814), translation by Margaret Hunt (1884).

Once upon a time there was a dear little girl who was loved by every one who looked at her, but most of all by her grandmother, and there was nothing that she would not have given to the child. Once she gave her a little cap of red velvet, which suited her so well that she would never wear anything else; so she was always called "Little Red-Cap." One day her mother said to her, "Come, Little Red-Cap, here is a piece of cake and a bottle of wine; take them to your grandmother, she is ill and weak, and they will do her good. Set out before it gets hot, and when you are going, walk nicely and quietly and do not run off the path, or you may fall and break the bottle, and then your grandmother will get nothing; and when you go into her room, don't forget to say, 'Good-morning,' and don't peep into every corner before you do it." "I will take great care," said Little Red-Cap to her mother, and gave her hand on it.

The grandmother lived out in the wood, half a league from the village, and just as Little Red-Cap entered the wood, a wolf met her. Red-Cap did not know what a wicked creature he was, and was not at all afraid of him. "Good-day, Little Red-Cap," said he. "Thank you kindly, wolf." "Whither away so early, Little Red-Cap?" "To my grandmother's." "What have you got in your apron?" "Cake and wine; yesterday was baking-day, so poor sick grandmother is to have something good, to make her stronger." "Where does your grandmother live, Little Red-Cap?" "A good quarter of a league farther on in the wood; her house stands under the three large oak-trees, the nut-trees are just below; you surely must know it," replied Little Red-Cap. The wolf thought to himself, "What a tender young creature! what a nice plump mouthful -- she will be better to eat than the old woman. I must act craftily, so as to catch both."

So he walked for a short time by the side of Little Red-Cap, and then he said, "See Little Red-Cap, how pretty the flowers are about here -- why do you not look round? I believe, too, that you do not hear how sweetly the little birds are singing; you walk gravely along as if you were going to school, while everything else out here in the wood is merry." Little Red-Cap raised her eyes, and when she saw the sunbeams dancing here and there through the trees, and pretty flowers growing everywhere, she thought, "Suppose I take grandmother a fresh nosegay; that would please her too. It is so early in the day that I shall still get there in good time;" and so she ran from the path into the wood to look for flowers. And whenever she had picked one, she fancied that she saw a still prettier one farther on, and ran after it, and so got deeper and deeper into the wood.

Meanwhile the wolf ran straight to the grandmother's house and knocked at the door. "Who is there?" "Little Red-Cap," replied the wolf. "She is bringing cake and wine; open the door." "Lift the latch," called out the grandmother, "I am too weak, and cannot get up." The wolf lifted the latch, the door flew open, and without saying a word he went straight to the grandmother's bed, and devoured her. Then he put on her clothes, dressed himself in her cap, laid himself in bed and drew the curtains.

Little Red-Cap, however, had been running about picking flowers, and when she had gathered so many that she could carry no more, she remembered her grandmother, and set out on the way to her. She was surprised to find the cottage-door standing open, and when she went into the room, she had such a strange feeling that she said to herself, "Oh dear! how uneasy I feel to-day, and at other times I like being with grandmother so much." She called out, "Good morning," but received no answer; so she went to the bed and drew back the curtains.

There lay her grandmother with her cap pulled far over her face, and looking very strange. "Oh! grandmother," she said, "what big ears you have!" "The better to hear you with, my child," was the reply. "But, grandmother, what big eyes you have!" she said. "The better to see you with, my dear." "But, grandmother, what large hands you have!" "The better to hug you with." "Oh! but, grandmother, what a terrible big mouth you have!" "The better to eat you with!" And scarcely had the wolf said this, than with one bound he was out of bed and swallowed up Red-Cap.

When the wolf had appeased his appetite, he lay down again in the bed, fell asleep and began to snore very loud.

The huntsman was just passing the house, and thought to himself, "How the old woman is snoring! I must just see if she wants anything." So he went into the room, and when he came to the bed, he saw that the wolf was lying in it. "Do I find thee here, thou old sinner!" said he. "I have long sought thee!" Then just as he was going to fire at him, it occurred to him that the wolf might have devoured the grandmother, and that she might still be saved, so he did not fire, but took a pair of scissors, and began to cut open the stomach of the sleeping wolf.

When he had made two snips, he saw the little Red-Cap shining, and then he made two snips more, and the little girl sprang out, crying, "Ah, how frightened I have been! How dark it was inside the wolf;" and after that the aged grandmother came out alive also, but scarcely able to breathe.

Red-Cap, however, quickly fetched great stones with which they filled the wolf's body, and when he awoke, he wanted to run away, but the stones were so heavy that he fell down at once, and fell dead. Then all three were delighted. The huntsman drew off the wolf's skin and went home with it; the grandmother ate the cake and drank the wine which Red-Cap had brought, and revived, but Red-Cap thought to herself, "As long as I live, I will never by myself leave the path, to run into the wood, when my mother has forbidden me to do so."

The Maïeutics for Little Red Riding Hood

In the tale of Little Red Riding Hood, the focus is not on biological fertilization, even if there is once again a single individual cut in two halves, as in Þrymskviða (see: *Paganism explained Part I*), but on the reincarnation of the ancestor in the weaned child (the seven years old child).

There are several versions of the tale. It should be noted that in the Chinese version, it is the grandmother who will visit her three girls. But here again, it does not change the meaning.

Little Red Riding Hood, in some versions, comes from her mother's house, and in others she has just finished working on a farm with cows. This detail is reminiscent of the tale of Jack and the beanstalk and indicates that the child we are talking about is just weaned.

The child brings to her grandmother a gift that her mother gave her, or that she got as paiment for looking after the cows. It is in principle the same, in both cases we have the image of the mother (the cow is the avatar of the mother).

This gift changes depending on the versions, but it is usually a milky or red drink, like wine, and a round cake or bread. Here we have a clear symbol of the placenta.

Little Red Riding Hood is the fetus, or the future fetus. That's why she is red, and she wears a hat, even if some versions don't retain this detail, the fact that it was kept in the artistic representations and to designate the tale signals that it is relatively important. The hat is always the amniotic bag, the headdress of the fetus. In some versions, the Red Riding Hood has no gender, we don't know if it's a girl or a boy. In French, she is called "fillon-fillette" ("boy-girl").

This is due to the fact that we don't know the gender of the fetus, but also to the symbol of the seven-year-old child, who is not yet clearly of either gender, is by default often female. The fetus and the seven-year-old are equivalent symbols.

She meets the wolf, that is to say the female genitals. The female genitals and the uterus. The female reproductive system, so to speak.

It is not always a wolf, in some French versions, it is a *bzou,* that means a werewolf (so clearly the grandmother voluntarily transformed into a wolf), or an ugly man (image of the dead ancestor), or an ogress, like in the Italian version: see *The false Grandmother (La finta nonna)* by Italo Calvino in Italian Folktales (1956). Because of copyrights, the Italian version could not be included in full in this book.

In the Italian version, the little girl does not meet this ogress before her arrival at the (fake) grandmother's home. Leaving her mother's house because his mother needs to borrow the sifter of the grandmother (*the placenta,* the mother needs *a placenta* to *sift* flour), she meets the River and asks it to let her pass. The river replies that for this it must give it her ring-shaped cakes. The ring-shaped cake is the image of the cervix. As the coin given to Charon to pass the Styx, it is essential. The coin, more precisely represents the egg, which one must have to access the kingdom of the dead, and that we obtain symbolically in the ritual of reincarnation in exchange for the milk teeth. The egg, the coin, are therefore the adult teeth, seeds growing in the child.

Some say that I pretend things that do not make sense, but you are wrong, I don't give any symbols without reason. The wolf or dog, in all European mythology, is the female reproductive system. This symbol, like all the other symbols that I explain, works in all cases, with all the myths, with all the tales, with all the traditions.

In the version *"The girl and the wolf"*, Little Red Riding Hood can choose between the path of pins or the path of needles, in other words always something that stings, like the umbilical cord, of which one of the most avatars common is also the spear.

The wolf shows the way to the ancestor, you must remember that it is a reincarnation. Obviously, he takes the shortest path, because he already has the ancestor in him, he himself contains the ancestor. He rules in is own house. The image of someone eaten is the same as that of someone in the womb, remember it. The wolf eats as the uterus eats. The wolf makes the link between the ancestor and the child.

The moment of the opening of the house is often accompanied by a magic phrase or behavior, given by the ancestor or sometimes the mother (because there is a strong analogy between the right to enter the egg and the right to be accepted in this symbolic pregnancy.): ***"Pull the bobbin, and the latch will go up."*** or ***"don't forget to say, 'Good-morning,' and don't peep into every corner before you do it."***.

This is the password. The house is also an avatar of the uterus and the grave, as well as the bed, more precisely.

When the child arrives, the wolf grandmother offers him food. We must insist on that. It is the child who brings food (brings with him the placenta), but it is he who is fed by the wolf grandmother. It is the wolf that is hungry, and yet it feeds the child-fetus. The grandmother-wolf takes its classic role of placenta (the placenta and the ancestor are equivalent in most myths, it is the ancestor who transmits the knowledge to his new body). She gives the child blood and meat to eat. It is stated in most ancient versions that this blood and meat are those of the grandmother, partially devoured by the wolf. Often, the child eats it, and then it is warned by birds (especially the hormones, Hermes with wings-feet is the father of Pan, but also the placenta and its wings-amniotic bag itself, which is why birds are often in a tree: the placenta) that she is devouring her grandmother. In some versions, the girl sees the grandmother's teeth in the meat and blood, or in the pan, and this repels her (we will see in the analyzes of the following tales how the teeth are an important symbol).

There I must mention the Italian version:

"Grandmother, Mamma wants the sifter."

"It's late now. I'll give it to you tomorrow. Come to bed."

"Grandmother, I'm hungry, I want my supper first."

"Eat the beans boiling in the boiler."

In the pot were the teeth. The child stirred them around and said, "Grandmother, they're too hard."

Often the baby goes to bed with her sick (dead) grandmother, but she begins to doubt. These two symbols refer to the ready fetus who wants to go out. In a way, it becomes aware of itself and sees itself as a cannibal who eats the blood (or the milk) of his mother, here in the tale. That means it becomes an individual.

Often, she asks to pee. The wolf tells her to do in bed (as all fetuses do, since they pee in the amniotic bag), but she says it's dirty. In the local French version from Touraine presented before, as in the Italian, the wolf hooks her to a rope, to let her out to pee, while being able to recall her by pulling on the rope (of course the umbilical cord).

She leaves the house, and when the wolf is worried about not seeing her come back, it's too late, she doesn't come back (sometimes some hormone-birds tricks him, imitating the girl's voice), and this wolf-shaped grandmother (that means the ancestor in the womb: in the placental form) comes out afterwards. The umbilical cord was cut, she has been (re)born.

In the version from Touraine, it is not a wolf, but an old gentleman (the ancestor) with a sow (the sow is a slightly rarer avatar of the placenta and the amniotic bag: she searches and scratches the soil looking for food as the placenta scratches the womb in search of food, and she herself is food). He goes out after the little girl, and meets some washer women (the midwives). He asks them if they saw a "boy-girl" with a dog that followed her. They say yes, they have spread white cloths over the water, and she passed over them. The gentleman also passes on these linens with his sow, and as he drowns (loses his breath) he tells his sow to lap, to lick in as much as she can, otherwise they will both drown. This is the image of the placenta that comes out after the fetus, with the cord beating like the heart. After the release of the placenta, the cord stops beating and thus the placenta and its cord literally lose their breath and die, drowning in the water of the amniotic bag and in their blood.

The Brothers Grimm version is interesting, of course, with regard to the symbols of birth, since the hunter opens the belly and brings out the little girl, and then the grandmother who is barely breathing. She says she was very scared, which is one of the characteristics of the end of a childbirth, adrenaline being essential to the final push, as explained in details in *The Secret of the She-Bear,* reason why the god Pan / Loki / Faunus / Cernunnos (...) is so important, so scary, and especially so misunderstood...

The hunter symbol will be included in other books. Some authors say that the hunter was invented by the Grimm brothers, because it does not appear in any of the local versions known *today*. I don't think so, because it is actually present in several local versions in the form of one or several *woodcutters* that scare the wolf, and also in the form of washers (midwives). The hunter and the woodcutter are equivalent symbols: in both cases they are the ones who give birth and deliver (cut) from the placenta-tree. They are the priest, the druid, the sorcerer, the midwife, and the ancestor and placenta itself.

The stones in the Grimm versions are the blood, the blood clots, like the ice or stone ettins in Þrymskviða.

Let's go back to the symbol of the female genitals. We will talk about Cerberus or Garm (the one who is stained, stained with blood), Geri and Freki the wolves of Óðinn, Fenrir, and quickly Anubis, but there are others, like the mother mother of Romulus and Remus and Culann's dog.

Well, already, how not to connect vulva and wulf (ulv in Norwegian)? But that's not all. If we see at etymology, the name *varg* (wolf), comes from *virgo, virges,* the same word as *virgin,* which does not mean what one believes, but *"who swells"*, this root gave the word *vigueur* (force) in French. But what is swelling, if not the female reproductive system, the uterus (and the fetus and egg, or the amniotic bag, which is, in fact, *Freyja, Aphrodite,* the true *"virgin"*).

Even today, if you look for a bit, you can find that we use the same words.

Often, this dog has three heads, or two and sometimes only one. It can similarly be two or three dogs. These are *labia majora, labia minora* and *the cervix,* or *the vulva* and *cervix*. Geri and

Freki mean respectively "hungry" and "hard", hungry like a pregnant's belly, and hard as a pregnant's belly. They eat Óðinn's food while he receives only wine (the mother eats the food and the fetus receives her blood. The wine is always the avatar of blood). Cerberus must be hidden (like the female genitals), and he is put to sleep several times with a poisoned cake, or sometimes a cake dipped in poisoned wine. Of course it is the placenta, which puts the mother to sleep and tricks her thanks to the hormones, so that she agrees to keep a being originally partly foreign to her body. It should be noted that the mother's immune system is considerably lowered during pregnancy by placental hormones, so that the body does not reject the fetus.

Fenrir (*wet and closed place*) is attached by the link Gleipnir. He is also tricked to be tied up. I'm sure you're wondering what it is, this famous link.

It is the *linea nigra*:

The *linea nigra* appears in 75% of pregnancies, it is produced by a hormone secreted by the placenta. It literally *attaches* the female genitals, ranging from pubis to navel, turning around the navel, to sometimes continue further.

And, of course, there is also Anubis, the god who chooses, who enters the realm of the dead, and the one who embalms and packs the dead...

The fact that a moral has been added to tales, especially in the 17th century, is unfortunately a sign that the tale, already at that time, had lost its meaning, at least for those who transcribed it. This desire to explain the tale in this way is probably related to wanting to explain the terrible symbols of cannibalism, murder, etc. In old and original versions of the classic tales (which have gradually been softened), these symbols are indeed shocking and incomprehensible if one does not grasp the quintessence of the tale. In my opinion, their shocking aspect is quite voluntary, aiming precisely at pushing the one who hears the tale to understand the real meaning of the tale (see the Socrates maieutic technique, explained in *The Secret of the She-Bear*).

Jack and the Beanstalk

As recorded by Joseph Jacobs, *English Fairy Tales* (1890)

There was once upon a time a poor widow who had an only son named Jack, and a cow named Milky-White. And all they had to live on was the milk the cow gave every morning, which they carried to the market and sold. But one morning Milky-White gave no milk, and they didn't know what to do.

"What shall we do, what shall we do?" said the widow, wringing her hands.

"Cheer up, mother, I'll go and get work somewhere," said Jack.

"We've tried that before, and nobody would take you," said his mother. "We must sell Milky-White and with the money start a shop, or something."

"All right, mother," says Jack. "It's market day today, and I'll soon sell Milky-White, and then we'll see what we can do."

So he took the cow's halter in his hand, and off he started. He hadn't gone far when he met a funny-looking old man, who said to him, "Good morning, Jack."

"Good morning to you," said Jack, and wondered how he knew his name.

"Well, Jack, and where are you off to?" said the man.

"I'm going to market to sell our cow there."

"Oh, you look the proper sort of chap to sell cows," said the man. "I wonder if you know how many beans make five."

"Two in each hand and one in your mouth," says Jack, as sharp as a needle.

"Right you are," says the man, "and here they are, the very beans themselves," he went on, pulling out of his pocket a number of strange-looking beans. "As you are so sharp," says he, "I don't mind doing a swap with you -- your cow for these beans."

"Go along," says Jack. "Wouldn't you like it?"

"Ah! You don't know what these beans are," said the man. "If you plant them overnight, by morning they grow right up to the sky."

"Really?" said Jack. "You don't say so."

"Yes, that is so. And if it doesn't turn out to be true you can have your cow back."

"Right," says Jack, and hands him over Milky-White's halter and pockets the beans.

Back goes Jack home, and as he hadn't gone very far it wasn't dusk by the time he got to his door.

"Back already, Jack?" said his mother. "I see you haven't got Milky-White, so you've sold her. How much did you get for her?"

"You'll never guess, mother," says Jack.

"No, you don't say so. Good boy! Five pounds? Ten? Fifteen? No, it can't be twenty."

"I told you you couldn't guess. What do you say to these beans? They're magical. Plant them overnight and -- "

"What!" says Jack's mother. "Have you been such a fool, such a dolt, such an idiot, as to give away my Milky-White, the best milker in the parish, and prime beef to boot, for a set of paltry beans? Take that! Take that! Take that! And as for your precious beans here they go out of the window. And now off with you to bed. Not a sup shall you drink, and not a bit shall you swallow this very night."

So Jack went upstairs to his little room in the attic, and sad and sorry he was, to be sure, as much for his mother's sake as for the loss of his supper.

At last he dropped off to sleep.

When he woke up, the room looked so funny. The sun was shining into part of it, and yet all the rest was quite dark and shady. So Jack jumped up and dressed himself and went to the window. And what do you think he saw? Why, the beans his mother had thrown out of the window into the garden had sprung up into a big beanstalk which went up and up and up till it reached the sky. So the man spoke truth after all.

The beanstalk grew up quite close past Jack's window, so all he had to do was to open it and give a jump onto the beanstalk which ran up just like a big ladder. So Jack climbed, and he climbed, and he climbed, and he climbed, and he climbed, and he climbed, and he climbed till at last he reached the sky. And when he got there he found a long broad road going as straight as a dart. So he walked along, and he walked along, and he walked along till he came to a great big tall house, and on the doorstep there was a great big tall woman.

"Good morning, mum," says Jack, quite polite-like. "Could you be so kind as to give me some breakfast?" For he hadn't had anything to eat, you know, the night before, and was as hungry as a hunter.

"It's breakfast you want, is it?" says the great big tall woman. "It's breakfast you'll be if you don't move off from here. My man is an ogre and there's nothing he likes better than boys broiled on toast. You'd better be moving on or he'll be coming."

"Oh! please, mum, do give me something to eat, mum. I've had nothing to eat since yesterday morning, really and truly, mum," says Jack. "I may as well be broiled as die of hunger."

Well, the ogre's wife was not half so bad after all. So she took Jack into the kitchen, and gave him a hunk of bread and cheese and a jug of milk. But Jack hadn't half finished these when thump! thump! thump! the whole house began to tremble with the noise of someone coming.

"Goodness gracious me! It's my old man," said the ogre's wife. "What on earth shall I do? Come along quick and jump in here." And she bundled Jack into the oven just as the ogre came in.

He was a big one, to be sure. At his belt he had three calves strung up by the heels, and he unhooked them and threw them down on the table and said, "Here, wife, broil me a couple of these for breakfast. Ah! what's this I smell?

Fee-fi-fo-fum,
I smell the blood of an
Englishman,
Be he alive, or be he dead,
I'll have his bones to grind
my bread."

"Nonsense, dear," said his wife. "You're dreaming. Or perhaps you smell the scraps of that little boy you liked so much for yesterday's dinner. Here, you go and have a wash and tidy up, and by the time you come back your breakfast'll be ready for you."

So off the ogre went, and Jack was just going to jump out of the oven and run away when the woman told him not. "Wait till he's asleep," says she; "he always has a doze after breakfast."

Well, the ogre had his breakfast, and after that he goes to a big chest and takes out a couple of bags of gold, and down he sits and counts till at last his head began to nod and he began to snore till the whole house shook again.

Then Jack crept out on tiptoe from his oven, and as he was passing the ogre, he took one of the bags of gold under his arm, and off he pelters till he came to the beanstalk, and then he threw down the bag of gold, which, of course, fell into his mother's garden, and then he climbed down and climbed down till at last he got home and told his mother and showed her the gold and said, "Well, mother, wasn't I right about the beans? They are really magical, you see."

So they lived on the bag of gold for some time, but at last they came to the end of it, and Jack made up his mind to try his luck once more at the top of the beanstalk. So one fine morning he rose up early, and got onto the beanstalk, and he climbed, and he climbed, and he climbed, and he climbed, and he climbed, and he climbed till at last he came out onto the road again and up to the great tall house he had been to before. There, sure enough, was the great tall woman a-standing on the doorstep.

"Good morning, mum," says Jack, as bold as brass, "could you be so good as to give me something to eat?"

"Go away, my boy," said the big tall woman, "or else my man will eat you up for breakfast. But aren't you the youngster who came here once before? Do you know, that very day my man missed one of his bags of gold."

"That's strange, mum," said Jack, "I dare say I could tell you something about that, but I'm so hungry I can't speak till I've had something to eat."

Well, the big tall woman was so curious that she took him in and gave him something to eat. But he had scarcely begun munching it as slowly as he could when thump! thump! they heard the giant's footstep, and his wife hid Jack away in the oven.

All happened as it did before. In came the ogre as he did before, said, "Fee-fi-fo-fum," and had his breakfast off three broiled oxen.

Then he said, "Wife, bring me the hen that lays the golden eggs." So she brought it, and the ogre said, "Lay," and it laid an egg all of gold. And then the ogre began to nod his head, and to snore till the house shook.

Then Jack crept out of the oven on tiptoe and caught hold of the golden hen, and was off before you could say "Jack Robinson." But this time the hen gave a cackle which woke the ogre, and just as Jack got out of the house he heard him calling, "Wife, wife, what have you done with my golden hen?"

And the wife said, "Why, my dear?"

But that was all Jack heard, for he rushed off to the beanstalk and climbed down like a house on fire. And when he got home he showed his mother the wonderful hen, and said "Lay" to it; and it laid a golden egg every time he said "Lay."

Well, Jack was not content, and it wasn't long before he determined to have another try at his luck up there at the top of the beanstalk. So one fine morning he rose up early and got to the beanstalk, and he climbed, and he climbed, and he climbed, and he climbed till he got to the top.

But this time he knew better than to go straight to the ogre's house. And when he got near it, he waited behind a bush till he saw the ogre's wife come out with a pail to get some water, and then he crept into the house and got into the copper. He hadn't been there long when he heard thump! thump! thump! as before, and in came the ogre and his wife.

"Fee-fi-fo-fum, I smell the blood of an Englishman," cried out the ogre. "I smell him, wife, I smell him."

"Do you, my dearie?" says the ogre's wife. "Then, if it's that little rogue that stole your gold and the hen that laid the golden eggs he's sure to have got into the oven." And they both rushed to the oven.

But Jack wasn't there, luckily, and the ogre' s wife said, "There you are again with your fee-fi-fo-fum. Why, of course, it's the boy you caught last night that I've just broiled for your breakfast. How forgetful I am, and how careless you are not to know the difference between live and dead after all these years."

So the ogre sat down to the breakfast and ate it, but every now and then he would mutter, "Well, I could have sworn --" and he'd get up and search the larder and the cupboards and everything, only, luckily, he didn't think of the copper.

After breakfast was over, the ogre called out, "Wife, wife, bring me my golden harp."

So she brought it and put it on the table before him. Then he said, "Sing!" and the golden harp sang most beautifully. And it went on singing till the ogre fell asleep, and commenced to snore like thunder.

Then Jack lifted up the copper lid very quietly and got down like a mouse and crept on hands and knees till he came to the table, when up he crawled, caught hold of the golden harp and dashed with it towards the door.

But the harp called out quite loud, "Master! Master!" and the ogre woke up just in time to see Jack running off with his harp.

Jack ran as fast as he could, and the ogre came rushing after, and would soon have caught him, only Jack had a start and dodged him a bit and knew where he was going.

When he got to the beanstalk the ogre was not more than twenty yards away when suddenly he saw Jack disappear like, and when he came to the end of the road he saw Jack underneath climbing down for dear life. Well, the ogre didn't like trusting himself to such a ladder, and he stood and waited, so Jack got another start.

But just then the harp cried out, "Master! Master!" and the ogre swung himself down onto the beanstalk, which shook with his weight. Down climbs Jack, and after him climbed the ogre.

By this time Jack had climbed down and climbed down and climbed down till he was very nearly home. So he called out, "Mother! Mother! bring me an axe, bring me an axe." And his mother came rushing out with the axe in her hand, but when she came to the beanstalk she stood stock still with fright, for there she saw the ogre with his legs just through the clouds.

But Jack jumped down and got hold of the axe and gave a chop at the beanstalk which cut it half in two. The ogre felt the beanstalk shake and quiver, so he stopped to see what was the matter. Then Jack gave another chop with the axe, and the beanstalk was cut in two and began to topple over. Then the ogre fell down and broke his crown, and the beanstalk came toppling after.

Then Jack showed his mother his golden harp, and what with showing that and selling the golden eggs, Jack and his mother became very rich, and he married a great princess, and they lived happy ever after.

As recorded by Andrew Lang, *The Red Fairy Book* (1890)

Once upon a time there was a poor widow who lived in a little cottage with her only son Jack. Jack was a giddy, thoughtless boy, but very kind hearted and affectionate. There had been a hard winter, and after it the poor woman had suffered from fever and ague. Jack did no work as yet, and by degrees they grew dreadfully poor.

The widow saw that there was no means of keeping Jack and herself from starvation but by selling her cow; so one morning she said to her son, "I am too weak to go myself, Jack, so you must take the cow to market for me, and sell her."

Jack liked going to the market to sell the cow very much; but as he was on the way, he met a butcher who had some beautiful beans in his hand. Jack stopped to look at them, and the butcher told the boy that they were of great value and persuaded the silly lad to sell the cow for these beans.

When he brought them home to his mother instead of the money she expected for her nice cow, she was very vexed and shed many tears, scolding Jack for his folly. He was very sorry, and mother and son went to bed very sadly that night; their last hope seemed gone.

At daybreak Jack rose and went out into the garden. "At least," he thought, "I will sow the wonderful beans. Mother says that they are just common scarlet runners, and nothing else; but I may as well sow them." So he took a piece of stick, and made some holes in the ground, and put in the beans.

That day they had very little dinner, and went sadly to bed, knowing that for the next day there would be none, and Jack, unable to sleep from grief and vexation, got up at day-dawn and went out into the garden.

What was his amazement to find that the beans had grown up in the night, and climbed up and up until they covered the high cliff that sheltered the cottage and disappeared above it! The stalks had twined and twisted themselves together until they formed quite a ladder.

"It would be easy to climb it," thought Jack. And, having thought of the experiment, he at once resolved to carry it out, for Jack was a good climber. However, after his late mistake about the cow, he thought he had better consult his mother first.

Wonderful Growth of the Beanstalk

So Jack called his mother, and they both gazed in silent wonder at the beanstalk, which was not only of great height, but was thick enough to bear Jack's weight. "I wonder where it ends," said Jack to his mother. "I think I will climb up and see."

His mother wished him not to venture up this strange ladder, but Jack coaxed her to give her consent to the attempt, for he was certain there must be something wonderful in the beanstalk; so at last she yielded to his wishes.

Jack instantly began to climb, and went up and up on the ladder-like beanstalk until everything he had left behind him -- the cottage, the village, and even the tall church tower -- looked quite little, and still he could not see the top of the beanstalk.

Jack felt a little tired, and thought for a moment that he would go back again; but he was a very persevering boy, and he knew that the way to succeed in anything is not to give up. So after resting for a moment he went on. After climbing higher and higher, until he grew afraid to look down for fear he should be giddy, Jack at last reached the top of the beanstalk, and found himself in a beautiful country, finely wooded, with beautiful meadows covered with sheep. A crystal stream ran through the pastures; not far from the place where he had got off the beanstalk stood a fine, strong castle.

Jack wondered very much that he had never heard of or seen this castle before; but when he reflected on the subject, he saw that it was as much separated from the village by the perpendicular rock on which it stood as if it were in another land.

While Jack was standing looking at the castle, a very strange looking woman came out of the wood, and advanced towards him. She wore a pointed cap of quilted red satin turned up with ermine. Her hair streamed loose over her shoulders, and she walked with a staff. Jack took off his cap and made her a bow.

"If you please, ma'am," said he, "is this your house?"

"No," said the old lady. "Listen, and I will tell you the story of that castle:"

Once upon a time there was a noble knight, who lived in this castle, which is on the borders of fairyland. He had a fair and beloved wife and several lovely children; and as his neighbours, the little people, were very friendly towards him, they bestowed on him many excellent and precious gifts.

Rumour whispered of these treasures; and a monstrous giant, who lived at no great distance, and who was a very wicked being, resolved to obtain possession of them.

So he bribed a false servant to let him inside the castle, when the knight was in bed and asleep, and he killed him as he lay. Then he went to the part of the castle which was the nursery, and also killed all the poor little ones he found there.

Happily for her, the lady was not to be found. She had gone with her infant son, who was only two or three months old, to visit her old nurse, who lived in the valley; and she had been detained all night there by a storm.

The next morning, as soon as it was light, one of the servants at the castle, who had managed to escape, came to tell the poor lady of the sad fate of her husband and her pretty babes. She could scarcely believe him at first, and was eager at once to go back and share the fate of her dear ones. But the old nurse, with many tears, besought her to remember that she had still a child, and that it was her duty to preserve her life for the sake of the poor innocent.

The lady yielded to this reasoning, and consented to remain at her nurse's house as the best place of concealment; for the servant told her that the giant had vowed, if he could find her, he would kill both her and her baby.

Years rolled on. The old nurse died, leaving her cottage and the few articles of furniture it contained to her poor lady, who dwelt in it, working as a peasant for her daily bread. Her spinning wheel and the milk of a cow, which she had purchased with the little money she had with her, sufficed for the scanty subsistence of herself and her little son. There was a nice little garden attached to the cottage, in which they cultivated peas, beans, and cabbages, and the lady was not ashamed to go out at harvest time, and glean in the fields to supply her little son's wants.

Jack, that poor lady is your mother. This castle was once your father's, and must again be yours.

Jack uttered a cry of surprise. "My mother! Oh, madam, what ought I to do? My poor father! My dear mother!"

"Your duty requires you to win it back for your mother. But the task is a very difficult one, and full of peril, Jack. Have you courage to undertake it?"

"I fear nothing when I am doing right," said Jack.

"Then," said the lady in the red cap, "you are one of those who slay giants. You must get into the castle, and if possible possess yourself of a hen that lays golden eggs, and a harp that talks. Remember, all the giant possesses is really yours." As she ceased speaking, the lady of the red hat suddenly disappeared, and of course Jack knew she was a fairy.

Jack determined at once to attempt the adventure; so he advanced, and blew the horn which hung at the castle portal. The door was opened in a minute or two by a frightful giantess, with one great eye in the middle of her forehead. As soon as Jack saw her he turned to run away, but she caught him, and dragged him into the castle.

"Ho, ho!" she laughed terribly. "You didn't expect to see me here, that is clear! No, I shan't let you go again. I am weary of my life. I am so overworked, and I don't see why I should not have a page as well as other ladies. And you shall be my boy. You shall clean the knives, and black the boots, and make the fires, and help me generally when the giant is out. When he is at home I must hide you, for he has eaten up all my pages hitherto, and you would be a dainty morsel, my little lad."

While she spoke she dragged Jack right into the castle. The poor boy was very much frightened, as I am sure you and I would have been in his place. But he remembered that fear disgraces a man, so he struggled to be brave and make the best of things.

"I am quite ready to help you, and do all I can to serve you, madam," he said, "only I beg you will be good enough to hide me from your husband, for I should not like to be eaten at all."

"That's a good boy," said the giantess, nodding her head; "it is lucky for you that you did not scream out when you saw me, as the other boys who have been here did, for if you had done so my husband would have awakened and have eaten you, as he did them, for breakfast. Come here, child; go into my wardrobe. He never ventures to open that. You will be safe there."

And she opened a huge wardrobe which stood in the great hall, and shut him into it. But the keyhole was so large that it admitted plenty of air, and he could see everything that took place through it. By and by he heard a heavy tramp on the stairs, like the lumbering along of a great cannon, and then a voice like thunder cried out.

Fe, fa, fi-fo-fum,
I smell the breath of an Englishman.
Let him be alive or let him be dead,
I'll grind his bones to make my bread.

"Wife," cried the giant, "there is a man in the castle. Let me have him for breakfast."

"You are grown old and stupid," cried the lady in her loud tones. "It is only a nice fresh steak off an elephant that I have cooked for you which you smell. There, sit down and make a good breakfast."

And she placed a huge dish before him of savoury steaming meat, which greatly pleased him and made him forget his idea of an Englishman being in the castle. When he had breakfasted he went out for a walk; and then the giantess opened the door, and made Jack come out to help her. He helped her all day. She fed him well, and when evening came put him back in the wardrobe.

The Hen That Lays Golden Eggs

The giant came in to supper. Jack watched him through the keyhole, and was amazed to see him pick a wolf's bone and put half a fowl at a time into his capacious mouth.

When the supper was ended he bade his wife bring him his hen that laid the golden eggs.

"It lays as well as it did when it belonged to that paltry knight," he said. "Indeed, I think the eggs are heavier than ever."

The giantess went away, and soon returned with a little brown hen, which she placed on the table before her husband. "And now, my dear," she said, "I am going for a walk, if you don't want me any longer."

"Go," said the giant. "I shall be glad to have a nap by and by."

Then he took up the brown hen and said to her, "Lay!" And she instantly laid a golden egg.

"Lay!" said the giant again. And she laid another.
"Lay!" he repeated the third time. And again a golden egg lay on the table.

Now Jack was sure this hen was that of which the fairy had spoken.

By and by the giant put the hen down on the floor, and soon after went fast asleep, snoring so loud that it sounded like thunder.

Directly Jack perceived that the giant was fast asleep, he pushed open the door of the wardrobe and crept out. Very softly he stole across the room, and, picking up the hen, made haste to quit the apartment. He knew the way to the kitchen, the door of which he found was left ajar. He opened it, shut and locked it after him, and flew back to the beanstalk, which he descended as fast as his feet would move.

When his mother saw him enter the house she wept for joy, for she had feared that the fairies had carried him away, or that the giant had found him. But Jack put the brown hen down before her, and told her how he had been in the giant's castle, and all his adventures. She was very glad to see the hen, which would make them rich once more.

The Money Bags

Jack made another journey up the beanstalk to the giant's castle one day while his mother had gone to market. But first he dyed his hair and disguised himself. The old woman did not know him again and dragged him in as she had done before to help her to do the work; but she heard her husband coming, and hid him in the wardrobe, not thinking that it was the same boy who had stolen the hen. She bade him stay quite still there, or the giant would eat him. Then the giant came in saying:

Fe, fa, fi-fo-fum,
I smell the breath of an Englishman.
Let him be alive or let him be dead,
I'll grind his bones to make my bread.

"Nonsense!" said the wife, "it is only a roasted bullock that I thought would be a tit-bit for your supper; sit down and I will bring it up at once."

The giant sat down, and soon his wife brought up a roasted bullock on a large dish, and they began their supper. Jack was amazed to see them pick the bones of the bullock as if it had been a lark.

As soon as they had finished their meal, the giantess rose and said:, "Now, my dear, with your leave I am going up to my room to finish the story I am reading. If you want me call for me."

"First," answered the giant, "bring me my money bags, that I may count my golden pieces before I sleep."

The giantess obeyed. She went and soon returned with two large bags over her shoulders, which she put down by her husband.

"There," she said; "that is all that is left of the knight's money. When you have spent it you must go and take another baron's castle."

"That he shan't, if I can help it," thought Jack.

The giant, when his wife was gone, took out heaps and heaps of golden pieces, and counted them, and put them in piles, until he was tired of the amusement. Then he swept them all back into their bags, and leaning back in his chair fell fast asleep, snoring so loud that no other sound was audible.

Jack stole softly out of the wardrobe, and taking up the bags of money (which were his very own, because the giant had stolen them from his father), he ran off, and with great difficulty descending the beanstalk, laid the bags of gold on his mother's table. She had just returned from town, and was crying at not finding Jack.

"There, mother, I have brought you the gold that my father lost."

"Oh, Jack! You are a very good boy, but I wish you would not risk your precious life in the giant's castle. Tell me how you came to go there again." And Jack told her all about it.

Jack's mother was very glad to get the money, but she did not like him to run any risk for her. But after a time Jack made up his mind to go again to the giant's castle.

So he climbed the beanstalk once more, and blew the horn at the giant's gate. The giantess soon opened the door. She was very stupid, and did not know him again, but she stopped a minute before she took him in. She feared another robbery; but Jack's fresh face looked so innocent that she could not resist him, and so she bade him come in, and again hid him away in the wardrobe.

By and by the giant came home, and as soon as he had crossed the threshold he roared out:

Fe, fa, fi-fo-fum,
I smell the breath of an Englishman.
Let him be alive or let him be dead,
I'll grind his bones to make my bread.

"You stupid old giant," said his wife, "you only smell a nice sheep, which I have grilled for your dinner."

And the giant sat down, and his wife brought up a whole sheep for his dinner. When he had eaten it all up, he said, "Now bring me my harp, and I will have a little music while you take your walk."

The giantess obeyed, and returned with a beautiful harp. The framework was all sparkling with diamonds and rubies, and the strings were all of gold.

"This is one of the nicest things I took from the knight," said the giant. "I am very fond of music, and my harp is a faithful servant."

So he drew the harp towards him, and said, "Play!" And the harp played a very soft, sad air. "Play something merrier!" said the giant. And the harp played a merry tune.

"Now play me a lullaby," roared the giant, and the harp played a sweet lullaby, to the sound of which its master fell asleep.

Then Jack stole softly out of the wardrobe, and went into the huge kitchen to see if the giantess had gone out. He found no one there, so he went to the door and opened it softly, for he thought he could not do so with the harp in his hand.

Then he entered the giant's room and seized the harp and ran away with it; but as he jumped over the threshold the harp called out, "Master! Master!" And the giant woke up. With a tremendous roar he sprang from his seat, and in two strides had reached the door.

But Jack was very nimble. He fled like lightning with the harp, talking to it as he went (for he saw it was a fairy), and telling it he was the son of its old master, the knight.

Still the giant came on so fast that he was quite close to poor Jack, and had stretched out his great hand to catch him. But, luckily, just at the moment he stepped upon a loose stone, stumbled, and fell flat on the ground, where he lay at his full length.

This accident gave Jack time to get on the beanstalk and hasten down it; but just as he reached their own garden he beheld the giant descending after him.

"Mother! mother!" cried Jack, "make haste and give me the axe." His mother ran to him with a hatchet in her hand, and Jack with one tremendous blow cut through all the stems except one.

"Now, mother, stand out of the way!" said he. Jack's mother shrank back, and it was well she did so, for just as the giant took hold of the last branch of the beanstalk, Jack cut the stem quite through and darted from the spot.

Down came the giant with a terrible crash, and as he fell on his head, he broke his neck, and lay dead at the feet of the woman he had so much injured.

Before Jack and his mother had recovered from their alarm and agitation, a beautiful lady stood before them. "Jack," said she, "you have acted like a brave knight's son, and deserve to have your inheritance restored to you. Dig a grave and bury the giant, and then go and kill the giantess."

"But," said Jack, "I could not kill anyone unless I were fighting with him; and I could not draw my sword upon a woman. Moreover, the giantess was very kind to me."

The fairy smiled on Jack. "I am very much pleased with your generous feeling," she said. "Nevertheless, return to the castle, and act as you will find needful."

Jack asked the fairy if she would show him the way to the castle, as the beanstalk was now down. She told him that she would drive him there in her chariot, which was drawn by two peacocks. Jack thanked her, and sat down in the chariot with her. The fairy drove him a long distance round, until they reached a village which lay at the bottom of the hill. Here they found a number of miserable-looking men assembled. The fairy stopped her carriage and addressed them.

"My friends," said she, "the cruel giant who oppressed you and ate up all your flocks and herds is dead, and this young gentleman was the means of your being delivered from him, and is the son of your kind old master, the knight."

The men gave a loud cheer at these words, and pressed forward to say that they would serve Jack as faithfully as they had served his father. The fairy bade them follow her to the castle, and they marched thither in a body, and Jack blew the horn and demanded admittance.

The old giantess saw them coming from the turret loop hole. She was very much frightened, for she guessed that something had happened to her husband; and as she came downstairs very fast she caught her foot in her dress, and fell from the top to the bottom and broke her neck.

When the people outside found that the door was not opened to them, they took crowbars and forced the portal. Nobody was to be seen, but on leaving the hall they found the body of the giantess at the foot of the stairs.

Thus Jack took possession of the castle. The fairy went and brought his mother to him, with the hen and the harp. He had the giantess buried, and endeavoured as much as lay in his power to do right to those whom the giant had robbed. Before her departure for fairyland, the fairy explained to Jack that she had sent the butcher to meet him with the beans, in order to try what sort of lad he was.

"If you had looked at the gigantic beanstalk and only stupidly wondered about it," she said, "I should have left you where misfortune had placed you, only restoring her cow to your mother. But you showed an inquiring mind, and great courage and enterprise, therefore you deserve to rise; and when you mounted the beanstalk you climbed the Ladder of Fortune."

She then took her leave of Jack and his mother.

The Maïeutics for Jack and the Beanstalk

In the two versions presented above, the tale begins with something about the cow of the family. Jack's mother is a widow and Jack is too young to work. They are poor, or they are so poor that they have nothing to eat at all. Either they have nothing to eat, and that is what makes them sell their cow, or the cow gives no more milk, and that is why they have no more to eat and why they must sell the cow. The lack of food is anyway related to the cow.

In fact, this is the sign of weaning. Jack is seven years old, he is biologically weaned. You must understand that in humans, the biological weaning is naturally at the latest at seven years (it is not an average, it is a maximum age). This is observed by the disappearance of the digestive enzyme of lactose (milk sugar): the lactase; the loss of the baby teeth, the weight ratio of the weaned child and adult compared to other mammals, and the maturity of the immune system.

In fact, the cow is an avatar of the nursing mother. Also note that the cow has exactly the same gestation time as the European woman: 280 days (10 moon months, or 9 solar months). Even today, breast milk is mainly replaced by cow's milk. The cow that has no more milk is the cow that weans, quite simply. It is also the image of parents who no longer have food in stories, they, or the mother, has no more milk to give. It is also the image of the parents or the mother who abandons her/their child or her/their children in the tales. She does not abandon them, she weans them. To abandon is simply an analogy of weaning, even more clearly when it is linked to a lack of food.

Weaning is *sevrer* in French, and it comes from the Latin *separare,* simply meaning *to separate*.

The seven years are in psychology the coming in *the age of reason,* and this marks an important change in the child, where he is more turned towards learning than to survival. This is the age of the reincarnation ritual described in *The Secret of the She-Bear.*

The fact that the father is dead is an image of the lost ancestor, of the lost self.

The moment Jack has to sell the cow and meet the old man is very important. This old man is the ancestor. It's Jack himself, ready to live again in himself. The mother wishes to have money for the cow, which is traditionally given against the baby teeth. The coins, I remind you, are the symbol of the ovum, the egg, in the ritual of reincarnation and the symbolic pregnancy and rebirth. In fact he receives money, he receives new teeth, the teeth of the ancestor. The coin *is* the teeth, they are equivalent symbols. You have to lose your baby teeth so that the ancestor comes back to you through the adult teeth. And adult teeth are like *seeds growing in the child*.

Teeth, in fact, are more than only teeth, teeth are directly related to brain development and maintenance. Be careful, I'm not saying that teeth are intelligence, but that teeth are related to the state of the brain. Thus, several studies highlight the link between chewing and memory or even cognitive abilities (*Gummed-up memory: chewing gum impairs short-term recall*, *Kozlov MD1, Hughes RW, Jones DM, 2012*). Similarly, to get rid of obsessing music, a study shows that it is good to chew (in this case chewing gum): *Want to block earworms from conscious awareness? B(u)y gum!, Beaman CP1, Powell K, Rapley E., 2015.*

Chewing will not make you directly smarter in the long term, but not chewing will degenerate your brain. This is what a Japanese study showed:

The study involved more than 1,500 elderly people in Japan who had their health monitored between 2007 and 2012.

The study found participants with fewer teeth had a greater chance of developing dementia within the five years of the study.

For example, people with 1-9 teeth had an 81% higher risk of dementia than those with 20 teeth or more.

Takeuchi K, Ohara T, Furuta M et al, Tooth Loss and Risk of Dementia in the Community: the Hisayama Study. The Journal of the American Geriatrics Society. Published online March 8 2017.

Well, I do not advertise chewing gums, it concerns any chewing. Chewing is related to the proper functioning of the brain. Healthy teeth support a healthy brain.

But in fact, why do I talk to you about teeth? He has not received teeth, he has received beans... You will quickly understand why teeth and beans are equivalent symbols.

You have to take all these stories as riddles.

Already, remember the Italian version of Little Red Riding Hood:

"Grandmother, I'm hungry, I want my supper first."

"Eat the beans boiling in the boiler."

In the pot were the teeth. The child stirred them around and said, "Grandmother, they're too hard."

Then you have to understand that the beans are seeds, and what do the seeds do? They grow. Like the teeth. Beans are also the replacements of the coins here, and the coins, as explained before, are notably avatars of the teeth (that is why the little mouse or the tooth fairy gives you coins in exchange for the baby/milk teeth). But that's not all. As explained in *The Secret of the She-Bear,* there are other traditions, where the teeth are replaced by coins or seeds, such as the tradition of the King Cake. The tradition is that one conceals a bean or a coin in a cake that will be shared, and the child who eats the piece with the bean is designated king or queen. In fact it is a reminiscence of the beginning of the reincarnation ritual. The child did not find a bean, but he lost his teeth in the cake/food.

Beans are all that makes up the intelligence, the specificity and the complexity of this tale. Yes, the teeth / beans given by the ancestor as payment against weaning (the sale of the nursing cow: Milky-White) are magical, they will grow in him and give him the knowledge of the ancestor, the identity of the ancestor. The so-called definitive teeth or adult teeth are not adult teeth, they are the teeth of the ancestors, growing in the mouth of the child, which becomes at that time more reasonable, more individual, and with a more marked personality, because the impulsive period related to strict survival has passed. This is the age of reason, starting around 7 years old and ending around 8 years old.

I will focus, for analysis, most on Andrew Lang's version, which is less known but more complete. In both versions, the beans, even if the mother does not believe in their magic, are planted either by mistake or by Jack. In both versions, Jack is hungry and is more or less rejected by his mother, the best images possible for weaning.

Let's say immediately that the bean and its huge stem, or rather its stems, twisted to each other, are an image of the placenta and the umbilical cord, which itself is linked, *in the world outside,* to the sky and to trees (see *The Secret of the She-Bear*). Jack entered the reincarnation ritual of our ancestors after weaning, and now he is learning from his ancestor, pictured by the father, through ***the placenta, who is genetically mostly the father.*** Jack wonders how he did not know this castle and this world before but understands that since it was so far away vertically, he did not realize its presence before. Here we have the clear image of the child who becomes aware, in this case, of his past, of the knowledge of himself as an ancestor. Distant vertically here, means distant in time. Jack learns, and remembers.

The fairy, as explained in *The Secret of the She-bear,* is the bee, the midwife of Nature, the one who helps plants give birth to their fruit, the one that helps to give birth to oneself, one's new identity, she is the goddess Maïa (see *the maieutics* of Socrates). **She is also the substitute of the ancestor in life, the one who keeps the knowledge and the passwords, and the one who keeps closed or opens.** On the other hand, she does not really have any power, she can only tell, explain, give her knowledge, ask questions and wait. The one who holds the power is the individual itself, it is he who alone can actually give birth to his identity, the ancestor, his reminiscence, his knowledge. That's why the fairy tells Jack that he has to do exactly as she tells him, otherwise she will lose her power and will not be able to help him any more.

Jack learns who he is, where he comes from, in a way as *Perceval*, he learns his name.

It is the ogre who killed the father and took all his possessions because that is what the placenta (which is also the dragon in tales and myths) does. The placenta is the father, the remains of the father, *in other words, the ancestor,* and the one who will transfer his remains, his memory, his brain, to his new body.

So he has the courage to challenge the ogre. The ogre is the male bear, but it is also the placenta in its dangerous side (*The Secret of the She-Bear*), the placenta is the one that receives food from the mother (the ogress), that's why it is she who prepares the dishes for him in tales, even if it is sometimes the ogre who hunts the animals (he is the hunter: he goes for the prepared food / blood himself, what is known today, since the placenta is even able to regulate the blood pressure of the mother -hence pregnancy diseases such as pre-eclampsia- that is to say, in other words: it can take more or less blood from the mother, and more or less quickly.). The ogre wants to eat the children because he hunts them (by the umbilical cord, sometimes also replaced by a spear or arrow), but also because he eats them literally, the placenta also pumping the deoxygenated («dirty») blood from the fetus to give it to the mother who «wash» and reoxygen it.

Of course, in the first proposed version of the tale (Jacobs'), Jack calls the ogress *«mum»*...

Like Óðinn, like the skull of the dead ancestor who has no eyes, like the bear, the ogre sees very badly, but he smells very well. Note that he says he smells *the breath (blood)* of an Englishman. Indeed, because he is connected to him by this breath through the umbilical cord, even if he can not see it. In the version by Lang, the ogress needs someone to help her tidy up and take care of her home (the uterus); in the version by Jacobs, Jack first asks to eat (like the fetus), and also gets something to eat, which is strange from *an ogress,* isn't it? Then he is hidden in the oven, not to be seen by the ogre male / placenta. The oven is the uterus, where the bread swells, is prepared and cooked. *Strange to accept being hidden in the oven of an ogress, right?*

In Lang's version, Jack will help the ogress to tidy, clean, and maintain the castle, as the fetus «maintains» the uterus. Note this quote: «Come here, child; go into my wardrobe. He never ventures to open *that.*». The uterus is the closed, secure, the strongest work in the world that even the father / placenta can not open. The keyhole, or cleft, present in several tales (*Donkey skin* for example), is the cervix, through where midwives can *see or feel* the fetus.

What is strange is that I tell you that the ogre is the placenta, but there, when Jack is hidden, he seems to be outside the womb. That's because the ogre / placenta is both the placenta (inside, it's actually inside the castle, like Jack when he cannot not see him) and the ancestor and the sorcerer / midwife (outside).

But in fact... the keyhole is also and especially *the navel,* Óðinn's one eye, that's why we can read the following in the Lang's version: *«But the keyhole was so large that it admitted plenty of air»*... And like the third eye, it is by this that Jack can «see»: *«and he could see everything that took place through it»*. In fact both are linked, the cord closing the uterus is the cervix, and/because the cut cord signifying the open uterus.

It is the ogre who hunts food, but it is his wife, the ogress, who prepares it. In other words, the placenta is seeking food (blood) prepared by the mother. The placenta, through the hormones, pushes the mother to eat, especially sweet foods, but it is the mother who turns this food into blood. Sometimes, in tales and in mythology, it is also the ogress who hunts. The ogre only eats meat, blood.

The ogress feeds Jack too. Strange, she's an ogress, but we almost never see her eating. It is precisely because for her *to eat is to transform the food, to prepare it*. This is also why the uterus is the oven. She, the pregnant woman, eats for the others: the placenta then the fetus. She prepares the food and for that she eats.

The chicken is, like birds in general, and often the birds with long neck (stork, goose, swan...: the neck being the umbilical cord), an image of the placenta and its amniotic bag.

In fact, all these objects that will parade in front of Jack (the chicken with the golden eggs, the bag of gold coins, the magic harp) are placenta avatars. As it has been explained in the book *The Secret of the Bear,* the ritual of reincarnation of our ancestors, which took place to the seven years of the child, lasted one year and it was composed of three pregnancies and symbolic births intertwined some in others. Thus, the classic tales are often formed on this model, with an action, a symbolic pregnancy and symbolic birth, repeated three times. As it involves three pregnancies and symbolic births, three avatars of the placenta are needed, which each time are feeding the fetus, giving him their knowledge, and then are dragged out with him at birth.

As in mythology, the attributes of a character are in fact an aspect of himself, they are used to give you a new information about him. It is a visual-spatial language. Here, it's the same thing. The main image of the placenta is the ogre, but his possessions are also himself. And also more interesting, you are told in the tale, that the placenta, and its possessions, are actually Jack's father. Interesting when we know today that the placenta is genetically predominantly the father, as said before:

Paternally expressed genes predominate in the placenta. *Wang X(1), Miller DC, Harman R, Antczak DF, Clark AG, 2013*

In fact, it's slightly more complicated. We can get a placenta when cloning, so with only maternal genes, but usually the placenta will not work, and if it works, we think that's why the clones are failing, because to give an image, the placenta thus obtained is «empty», it has no substance, it does not do its job, namely that of taking the nutrients from the mother to give them to the fetus. In fact, we obtain a completely defective fetus, even if genetically speaking it does not seem to be defective. It is thought that the placenta is mainly composed of the father's genes (if there are such genes), because evolutionarily speaking, it is an advantage. Yes, because it behaves *like an ogre*. The father has an interest in his fetus developing as much as possible. For the mother, it is more complicated because the fetus pumps in her reserves while he is partly «a foreign body». As a result, the body of the mother would tend not to give enough. *The placenta is literally the father in the mother, who pumps the mother's nutrients and even controls her body, to give them to the fetus.*

Placental developmental defects in cloned mammalian animals. *Ao Z(1), Liu DW(1), Cai GY(1), Wu ZF(1), Li ZC(1), 2016:*

«The cloning technique, also called somatic cell nuclear transfer (SCNT), has been successfully established and gradually applied to various mammalian species. However, the developmental rate of SCNT mammalian embryos is very low, usually at 1% to 5%, which limits the application of SCNT. Placental developmental defects are considered as the main cause of SCNT embryo development inhibition. Almost all of SCNT-derived mammalian placentas exhibit various abnormalities, such as placental hyperplasia, vascular defects and umbilical cord malformation. Mechanistically, these abnormalities result from failure of establishment of correct epigenetic modification in the trophectoderm genome, which leads to erroneous expression of important genes for placenta development-related, particularly imprinted genes. Consequently, aberrant imprinted

gene expression gives rise to placental morphologic abnormalities and functional defects, therefore decreases developmental competence of cloned embryos.»

You know what ? These famous nutrients, do you know where they are going? *Mainly to the brain (more than 60%).* That's why there is a disease of pregnancy which is peculiar to human, who has developed such a greedy brain. This is preeclampsia, the disease of the *a bit too greedy ogre*. Preeclampsia is, in short, a pregnancy-induced hypertension in the late pregnancy, caused by the placenta, which makes the mother's body work so much that it can be deadly for her. In any case, this is the way our ancestors saw this disease. Interestingly, when we know that the rare *born at term fetuses* from pre-eclamptic mothers have developed a larger brain than normal *born at-term fetuses*. Hypertension is simply more blood, faster, for the placenta, who wants to have more. As a result, for the mother's body, it is especially more work for the kidneys and the liver that must clean more blood, faster, and often these kidneys (and sometimes the liver) are failing and put the mother in a vital danger.

Moreover, only the birth and the exit of the placenta puts an end to the disease. But from the point of view of.... *the ogre,* it's perfect, *it's more to eat.*

This disease is associated with a greedy brain, and is only present in humans.

<u>Altered Fetal Head Growth in Preeclampsia</u>. *A Retrospective Cohort Proof-Of-Concept Study. Eviston DP(1), Minasyan A(2), Mann KP(3), Peek MJ(1), Nanan RK(2)., 2015:*

«A preeclamptic fetus born after 36.3 weeks gestation is estimated to have a larger head circumference than a control fetus, and this difference increases with increasing gestational age.»

All this to give you an image. *The placenta gives its head to the head of the fetus.* Often in tales, at the beginning of the story, the ogre is pretty tricky, and then over time, it's the child or children who gets smarter and who, in the end, get rid of the ogre by trickery. Clearly, he has become smarter over time. All this also to explain to you that the blood given to the fetus is also and above all what makes him intelligent, which gives him the possibility *to remember*. Blood is not only a physical element, but here, in this symbolic pregnancy, *a spiritual element,* it is the memory of the ancestor (here the father), the reminiscences, the understanding, transmitted by the placenta-ogre.

And this symbol is gold. Gold is blood and memory. Memory because gold is the oldest element (known) of the universe, it is thought that it is created in the death (explosion) of a star, and it does not alter. So, gold has seen everything from the beginning of our solar system. As our ancestors thought that, like with amnesiacs today, the objects of the past (the famous «gifts») allowed us to remember the knowledge of our past lives, what better than a object made of gold?

It's also music, because music is the language of the soul, it helps the soul to remember (that's why music can make you nostalgic), and is also breath, oxygen, so blood.

Let's go back to the story. Each time, the ogre eats a dish served by his wife, the pregnant woman (the pregnant woman is indeed the wife of the placenta, since the placenta is the father). And after, *only after,* he asks this one to bring him an avatar of himself who, (*dare I say it?*) *flows*. *After eating, the ogre / placenta flows,* blood / gold / music flows from him: he asks the hen to make eggs, he counts the gold coins from the bag (the amniotic bag), and he plays a tune of music with the harp (avatar of the bow, which pulls the arrow / umbilical cord). Meanwhile, Jack, the fetus, watches everything from the keyhole (the navel), understand: *he drinks,* like Óðinn from the well of Mímir, and finally, when the ogre / placenta falls asleep, he goes out through this hole, steals the blood / memory / knowledge / intelligence from the placenta / ogre (but which comes from his own father) and comes out of the womb with. In fact, the real thief in history is the fetus, but of course, since it was to him all his blood was destined. It is to him all these orgies benefit, it is to him that the substance of the ogre returns. Why is he gets rich then, you ask me? But because wealth is life, it is memory, it is spiritual knowledge and reminiscences.

Beware, this is not a glorification of fertility, it is a glorification of knowledge, deep knowledge of the world and nature, and of the voluntary transmission of the ancestor into a new body. I am often asked when I speak of reincarnation «but who was I? Who was you?». You probably will never know it. This is not what is important, it should not be misunderstood. *Reincarnation is taking possession of past knowledge, of deep knowledge of the functioning of Nature, of the universe and of its spiritual aspect.* This knowledge is particularly in the understanding of the myths and riddles that I present to you here. As in your life, all memories are not useful and therefore not kept. Otherwise you would be cluttered with useless memories... Likewise for past lives. Remember which individual you was, is it useful? No, not when there are so many things to remember as well.

Jack's tale ends in a very precious way for its understanding. At the end, the harp calls its master / ogre and so we understand that it and he are one. Thus, it also attracts him in his fall and death: birth.

But the best is this word game: Jack asks his mother to give him the axe (the axe as the hammer of Þórr, is an avatar of the heart), with the axe / heart, ***«in a tremendous blow»***, he cuts all the stems of the bean except one. Understand this as follows: ***in a stroke, but also in a breath,*** with the help of his heart (which will soon work alone and be the only one to give him oxygen, breath, blood) given by his mother, he breathes suddenly, and with that breath, he cuts off the blood circulation in the cord.

Note that the blood circulation stops by itself at birth, and that there remains then only the empty cord that connects the fetus to the mother. Theoretically, and contrary to modern practices, it is at this point that the cord should be cut. And there, what does he say to his mother? ***«Now, mother, stand out of the way!»*** And with the axe / heart, while the ogre / placenta holds the last branch (the cord), he cuts it, resulting in the fall and death of the placenta / ogre lying dead, near the mother, ***«the woman he had so much injured»***...:

«"Mother! mother!" cried Jack, "make haste and give me the axe." His mother ran to him with a hatchet in her hand, and Jack with one tremendous blow cut through all the stems except one.

"Now, mother, stand out of the way!" said he. Jack's mother shrank back, and it was well she did so, for just as the giant took hold of the last branch of the beanstalk, Jack cut the stem quite through and darted from the spot.

Down came the giant with a terrible crash, and as he fell on his head, he broke his neck, and lay dead at the feet of the woman he had so much injured.»

The image is particularly clear, you will agree...

Here, the image of the ogress who must also be killed, is the image of the pregnancy itself, the pregnant woman, the «possessed» aspect of the woman. Of course, she is now disappearing, with the death of her husband and her death is that of a placenta, of which she herself has become an aspect (*she breaks her neck,* her head is cut off, she is slaughtered: in tales that means *cutting the cord*).

The fairy is the midwife, the image of the mother herself (often she was the mother or grandmother of the mother). In fairy tales she is the god-mother, a role she often embodied before. She is also the witch, Maïa, the one who helps to give birth to knowledge, the one who keeps the passwords.

Other books by Varg Vikernes

-*Vargsmål*, Oslo 1997

-*Germansk Mytologi og Verdensanskuelse*, Stockholm 2000

-*Sorcery and Religion in Ancient Scandinavia*, London 2011

-*Reflections on European Mythology and Polytheism*, 2015

-*Mythic Fantasy Role-playing Game (MYFAROG)*, 2015

Other books by Marie Cachet

-*Le secret de l'Ourse*, 2016

-*Le besoin d'impossible*, 2009

Other Paganism Explained books:

-*Paganism Explained, Part I: Þrymskviða*

Made in the USA
Las Vegas, NV
26 August 2024